ON
KEEPING COMPANY WITH
MRS WOOLF

ON KEEPING COMPANY WITH MRS WOOLF

NEIL CURRY

All rights reserved. No part of this work covered by the copyright herein may be reproduced or used in any means – graphic, electronic, or mechanical, including copying, recording, taping, or information storage and retrieval systems – without written permission of the publisher.

Printed by imprintdigital
Upton Pyne, Exeter
www.digital.imprint.co.uk

Typesetting and cover design by narrator
www.narrator.me.uk
info@narrator.me.uk
033 022 300 39

Published by Shoestring Press
19 Devonshire Avenue, Beeston, Nottingham, NG9 1BS
(0115) 925 1827
www.shoestringpress.co.uk

First published 2018
© Copyright: Neil Curry
© Cover image: Sérgio Ninguém

The moral right of the author has been asserted.

ISBN 978-1-912524-07-5

ACKNOWLEDGEMENTS

Some of these poems first appeared in the following publications: *Poetry Ireland Review*, *The London Grip*, *Killing the Angel*, *The Virginia Woolf Bulletin*.

I would also like to acknowledge the peaceful hospitality of Buckfast Abbey where the sequence began.

A word dropped careless on a page
 May stimulate an eye,
When folded in perpetual seam
The wrinkled maker lie.

— Emily Dickinson

CONTENTS

On Beginnings	1
On The Family Album	2
On An Evening's Walk	4
On Parents	5
On St. Ives	6
On Sisters	7
On Social Occasions	8
On Leaving Things to Their Own Devices	9
On Love	10
On Killing the Angel	11
On An Encounter with Henry James	12
On Dreaming	13
On Sickness	14
On That Same Question	15
On Moving House	16
On London	17
On Going for a Walk	18
On Life in General	19
On The Gods	20
On Offering an Invitation	21
On Bookshops	22
On Reading	23
On Looking Out	24
On Words	25
On Some Brief Moments	26
On Not Writing	27
On The Ocean	28
On Not Managing to Read "The Waves"	29
On Keeping a Diary	30
On Letters	31
On Sir Leslie Stephen	32
On Things We've Forgotten	33
On Clio	34
On Reputations	35
On Railway Journeys	36
On Walking	37

On Events versus Ideas	38
On Expectation	39
On Mornings	40
On Particularities	41
On Servants	42
On Days	43
On The Association of Ideas	44
On Lytton Strachey	45
On Coping with Loss	46
On That Very Moment	47
On Nothing in Particular	48
On Listening	49
On Peace	50
On Air Raids	51
On Women and Two World Wars	52
On Endings	53
On Self-doubt	54
On Leonard Woolf	55
On Gardening	56
On Walking by the River	57

ON BEGINNINGS

Leastways, that's what I keep telling myself,
That it's going to begin soon, my real life:
That I will stride out onto centre stage
And face the limelight, engage in dialogue,
Deliver myself of a soliloquy,
Become the cynosure of every shining eye,
And exit to tumultuous applause.
But it's act three now, and waiting here in the wings
I fear I might not pick up on my cue.

ON
THE FAMILY ALBUM

By now, some of these pages
Tend to fall open of their own accord.
Look. *Julia Stephen, 1846–1895*.
I was twelve or thirteen then
And mother not yet fifty.

Sheer exhaustion I'd have put it down to.
Well, Father himself would have been
Quite enough, let alone the eight of us.
Raindrops fell; I couldn't manage tears.

***

And *Stella Duckworth*. She was twenty-eight.
Half-sister. It's such a silly term, isn't it?
Stella was more complete than any of us.

But coming home from her honeymoon, she felt
A little off-colour. A touch poorly.
Then the pains came. Appendicitis?
Peritonitis? *Hard to say*, they said.
Whichever it was, that dreadful man Seton
Botched it again. Three months
From bridal to deathbed, and her widower
Still not yet used to having been the groom.

***

Leslie Stephen. Sir Leslie, 1832–1904.
Look at the lovely beard.

It was a lingering and malicious cancer
Closed the life of 'our nation's biographer'.
Mercifully though: for how he would have loathed
The great age others had wished upon him.

***

Then, see, poor dear Thoby, at twenty-six,
Our golden boy, So tall, so talented,
And so beloved. We'd been on holiday
In Greece. Typhoid. I couldn't face
Breaking such news to Violet. Week
After week I lied to her. Kept up
A running fiction on his life,
And have, ever since, I sometimes
Do suspect, been lying to myself.

***

Tragic?
        Oh, yes; they took us seriously
In those days, the old gods.

ON
AN EVENING'S WALK

Threading our way through Russell Square
Under an enormous yellow moon
Beset and buffeted by London's clouds,
A yellow moon, which had risen over Persia,
It was not so much the urgent beauty
Of it, although on such an evening
That might well have been sufficient in itself,
No, it was the infinite oddity
Of it all, you said, so harassed one.

ON
PARENTS

It's odd though, for whereas your mother, as I recall
You telling me once, begrudged you squandering
Half-a-crown on a Penguin paperback,
(One of mine, I'd like to hope) conversely,
And almost from the day I first could read, I
Had total run of father's bookshelves.
Looking back, that does now seem to me
One of the weirdest—oh, you think wisest—
Decisions he could possibly have made.

ON ST. IVES

"A pocket paradise on the toenail
 Of England," your father called it. Sadly,
St. Ives is somewhere I've never been.
These days, I suspect, it's all fish and chips
And candyfloss and far too many people,
 But I'd have loved to have gone down there with you.
You'd have found room for me in Talland House?
That's kind. We could have played French cricket
Out on the lawn, walked along the sands
Together and heard the plaintive piping
Of the redshank. It might have been a bit
Intimidating, having to meet your parents:
My vowels would have been all wrong, I'm sure.
Well, if you say so. One could never fault
Or tire of the sound of the waves though,
Their growlings and susurrations; and theirs,
I think, the rhythm you've been struggling
So long to set words to. And the light, yes.
And the way the wind blew against the blind
 In your bedroom of a morning when you woke,
With so little then to suggest how your life
Would be lit by the beam from a lighthouse.

ON
SISTERS

Miss V. Stephen. That shared initial
Had you conjoined from the very outset I...

Not a bit of it.
I write; Vanessa paints.
And that in a family of writers, don't forget,
Where painting was rated pretty much on a par
With embroidery, or flower-arranging;
Something little girls were taught to do
By way of being 'an accomplishment'.
Canvas and paint are though, God bless us,
A far remove from paper and ink.

It sounds to me like you envy her somewhat.

Envy her? *Ut pictura poesis*, you mean?
Envy her? That one-dimensional silence?
My word, but you do come up with some odd ideas.

ON
SOCIAL OCCASIONS

For there she was. At the head of the stairs,
Nessa, a shimmer of sapphire, poised
To descend among those fragrant and
Oh-so-fragile ladies, who, as Thoby once observed,
Offered but the susurre of their silkeness
To one another. Somewhat gawky and gauche myself,
I had already managed to put one
Potential beau to flight (not that I'd
Meant to or minded much) by citing Plato,
But was it so very odd of me, do you think,
Wanting to ensconce myself in a little
Corner somewhere, where I could read
In Memoriam quietly to myself?

ON LEAVING THINGS TO THEIR OWN DEVICES

New people (it was inevitable)
Moved into Talland House and made it theirs.
Had it been up to me, I would have left it
To its own devices: let the lawns
Grow rank with dock and thistle; let the pots
Rust in the kitchen, spoons tarnish; let a slate
Shift on the roof so that cold winter rain
Might intrude, slowly peeling the patterned paper
From the walls and bringing with it the soft
Fur of fungus and rot to feed on rafter
And beam, loosen window frames and let the wind
In. I'd have it feel its age, totter and fall
As we all must. Entropy they call it, don't they?
Yes, I'd sooner have a wanderer
In some far-off time, coming across a few
Cut stones and an unexpected stand
Of lupin in the scrub, pause for a moment,
And wonder to himself whether or not
Some family might have dwelt there once.

ON
LOVE

Love. Whatever that means. Now it is quite nice
Having some spruced-up young man gaze at you
Through misty eyes and declare that he intends
To devote every moment of his life
To preserving you in a state of bliss,
But such circumstances tend to suggest
Very little of what he may actually be like.
After all, it was not until they first
Breakfasted together that a friend
Of a friend discovered that her husband
Repeatedly licked his forefinger
As he turned the pages of his morning paper.

ON
KILLING THE ANGEL

Coventry Patmore didn't invent her you know:
The Angel in the House; she'd dwelt
Among us for as long as we could remember,
Sweetly submissive and oh,
So unselfish—if there was a draught
She'd sit in it; chicken for supper and
She would have a leg. So sedate
And so demure, yet such a wet blanket too,
Countered each new turn we thought to take with
"Do you think you should, my dear?"
Then stopping us dead with,
"It would scarcely be lady-like." She had to go.
My word, yet she died hard.
But once we'd got her cornered,
Like Caesar in the Forum,
I just jabbed her in the jugular with my pen.

ON
AN ENCOUNTER WITH HENRY JAMES

With as many synonyms for the noun
Solemnity, as mind of man could conjure up,
He, Henry James, unsmilingly immaculate,
Came to a standstill on Oxford Street.
"Miss Stephen," (Was he, she wondered, about
To challenge her to a duel?) "I—that is—they
Tell me, yes—ahem—they tell me that you—
As indeed your father's daughter (slowly
His hat reoccupied his head) nay, your
Grandfather's grandchild, (And what a head)
The descendent—I may say—of a century
Of quill pens, of ink pots and, yes, of ink;
They tell me—ahum—in short, Miss Stephen, that you
Write." Now to have denied such an accusation,
And in a public place, struck her, she explained,
As altogether too churlish for words.

ON DREAMING

The moon was so very pale that night,
Pale as the necks of young girls on the beach
When they lift their hair for the heat—heat
Which had kept her slipping in and out of sleep, she said,
Sinking, then surfacing again, like something rotten
Floating down a river; and as she rolled
And turned in the flow, so she became aware
How crucial it was to grasp at the meaning
Of these images: the scythes, the towers,
The savages in the treetops. But, as ever,
The propinquity of so many wrinkled faces
Distracted her, as did the faint booming
Of some distant sea. And so her quest, alas, must needs
Begin again, while one by one the lights
Were coming on in the little town, and arm
In arm in the cool of the evening, mild-mannered
Couples came stepping out onto their terraces.

ON
SICKNESS

Sickness, much like the past, is another country,
Its customs unfamiliar, its dialect
(Beside which the language of love is infinite)
Keeps to itself, shuffles past, says nothing.
And what wastes we traverse to get there,
A land of insurgency, where the body,
Having no truck with armistice,
Asserts itself, subjects us to new laws.
Refugees who survive the long trek home
Choose not to talk about it; no poet
Having ever penned an epic on Malaria,
Or choral ode to his mistress, Influenza.

ON
THAT SAME QUESTION

Yes, that same question people put to us time and
Time again: *where* do you get your ideas from?
As if it were some kind of process.
A new idea? You either have it,
Or you don't; it's either there, or it's
Not there. It's like falling asleep; you can't
Catch yourself doing it. Now that's a phrase
I rather like the sound of—one I'll store away:
A new dress in my wardrobe, waiting
For some occasion when I can wear it.

ON
MOVING HOUSE

It was a warm and artless August afternoon
In the rose garden when we saw the chrysalis,
Grey, wrinkled and gnarled; saw it move,
And as it split, saw something come
Crawling out of it, tremulous and sticky,
Creased and damp. It clung there dazzled.
But we didn't wait to see it take to the air
On its vermilion and sugar-sprinkled wings,
No, we too (Well, if it can…) decamped and slammed
The door of that dark and narrow house behind us,
And came—to Bloomsbury, which, as you so rightly say,
Proved to be far more than simply a new address.

ON
LONDON

Now I might not go as far as Johnson
On that score, but I'd certainly agree
With Charles Lamb: London beats your Lake District
Hands down. Oh, come now. Face the facts, please.
Blencathra and Skiddaw look much the same
Today—give or take a passing cloud or two—
As they did on any day of last week. True?
Whereas Oxford Street is never the same street twice,
 Gaudy, bustling and vulgar though it might be.
Now my London is not your London, I know.
We had our motor cars and omnibuses,
 But horses still went clip-clop past our doors
And we had barrel-organs. Oh, yes,
 Didn't we just. We had barrel-organs!

ON
GOING FOR A WALK

I go out for a walk:

To get away from things:
                        and a myriad
Of other things demand my attention;
There wasn't a primrose there yesterday;
No leaves on the hawthorn yet of course.

To get some peace and quiet:
                        and there's the sound
Of raindrops pattering on the rim of my hat,
The whistle of the 4.30 train to Lewes,
And, oddly, I keep listening out for the woodpecker.

To get shot of other people:
                        yet here I am,
In no time at all, talking to myself.

ON
LIFE IN GENERAL

Sometimes it seems to me I live my life
Like a child at the circus, astounded
By the lions, the jugglers and the clowns,
The sequin-skirted tight-rope walker;
Speechless at the excitement and the
Glamour of it all; a speechlessness
I am dying to find words for.

ON
THE GODS

They scare me, they really do, those words
Of Dionysus at the close of *The Bacchae*:
"Why then evade what cannot be avoided?"
The threat. That authority. All the same,
I sometimes think we should have stuck with them,
The old gods. At least they were straight with us;
Would have us accept that things are as they are.
No child-like promises of paradise;
No, and no divine retribution either.
What's more, that we were made in their vengeful,
Lustful and bloody-minded image is an idea
I can quite happily go along with. Of course,
They did at times make the most terrible
Demands of us, and I don't just mean
The occasional ox, or the odd virgin,
You only have to think of Iphigenia…
When all's said and done though, they left us
Some wonderful stories, didn't they?

ON OFFERING AN INVITATION

Were you of a sudden to call out,
"Virginia!" which of your disparate
And unsettled selves would, I wonder,
Be the first to respond? No, do forgive me,
No such thought was in my mind. Nevertheless,
What I did have in mind to ask was which—
As you turned your head, conscious of their clamour,
And saw them gathered together in the doorway—
Which of all these several Virginias
Would you invite to come and sit beside you
In the firelight, at cocoa-time and share
The comfort of this Bach chorale?

ON
BOOKSHOPS

I have never knowingly, as Leonard
Once observed, walked past a secondhand bookshop,
Especially not those little ones down side streets
Where a bell hung in the door-jamb brings
Someone out from a back room. It is sobering,
And salutary too, to stand there
Among the homeless and the unwanted, the failed
And the forgotten. But chances are you'll catch sight of
Some old chums to smile at, or nod to:
Cowper or Gilbert White. And possibly even find,
Fallen down behind some fat volumes
Of Bulwer-Lytton, a titled lady
Eager to explain to you what goes on
Inside a beehive, or what it was like
To lie out under the stars with the Bedouin.
And on a high shelf there may be someone
Who, for reasons and in ways you never could
Have guessed, will become one of your best
And closest friends, and as (who was it?) said:
"In thy most need go by thy side."

ON
READING

"Choose an author as you choose a good friend,"
Said Sir Christopher Wren, but some choose us,
Just as some books read us, and change us
As they themselves change—the way people do—
When we read them, and such complicity
May come about as leaves us, on turning
To the last page, a little bemused maybe, yet eager
To begin writing it out all over again.

ON
LOOKING OUT

There are times when I get up and look
Out of the window, and it's as if
I'd been summoned; one might almost say
Told to. The hollyhocks, the lobelia
And the canna lilies haven't all been
Simply loafing about until roused up
By my attention. No, *mind*
Is a sort of susceptibility.
I'm quoting here. Our understanding
Dependent upon our participation,
The world's intelligibility realized.

ON
WORDS

They've been around
         far too long and
                gotten streetwise.
There's no telling
        where they've been
               —in God's house,
The playhouse,
        the whorehouse,
                and now in your house.
And no way of knowing
        whose mouth
               they've been in.
No, let's face it,
        there's just no
               trusting them.

ON
SOME BRIEF MOMENTS

In Kingsway this afternoon,
I saw a beggar woman,
Cuddling a little brown mongrel.
Blind she was and old.

She was sitting with her back against the wall,
And singing—singing quietly to herself,
As a fire engine went past.

I just thought they might
Be of interest to you,
These bright, though brief
Little moments of being.

ON
NOT WRITING

What was it like? Well, as she told
Her kindly, blank-faced old confidante
Of a diary, it was like teetering
On the very narrowest of pavements
Over a vast abyss, a pavement as thin
As the glaze of ice on a March pond.
Looking down made her dizzy and sick.
How could her fingers manage, she wondered,
To tolerate so much non-scribbling?

ON THE OCEAN

"What I find so tiresome about the ocean,"
 Someone once remarked to me, "is that
There are no flowers in it." So I wrote *The Waves*.

> *The waves broke*
> *And spread swiftly*
> *Over the shore*
> *One after another;*
> *Massed themselves and fell,*
> *Withdrew and fell again,*
> *Like the thud*
> *Of a great beast stamping.*

ON MY
NOT MANAGING TO READ
"THE WAVES"

Down on the lowest level
Of the cliff-face gardens of the Villa dei Pini
(It's at Bogliasco on the Ligurian coast)
I don't quite know how to tell you this,
Virginia, but I'll risk it nonetheless—
As I say, on the lowest level—
You get there down a steep and narrow
Twisting path between sabre-toothed cacti
And dark pines to where three great trees
Lean out so far they've had to be tied back
To the land to stop them rushing out
To paddle their old roots in the sea.
Then at the very lowest level of all there's this
Sudden little patch of lawn in bright sunlight
And a bench waiting for you in the shade
Of an olive tree.
                I'd taken a copy
Of *The Waves* to read there, but never
Got round to as much as opening it.
Even your words, Virginia, could not compete
With the actuality of the way they came
Pounding their fists against the rocks, then chuckling
To themselves ("We didn't really mean it.")
As they went meekly shuffling out again.

ON
KEEPING A DIARY

As Hamlet had Horatio, so I
Have my diary, someone to talk to,
My "poor servant ever"; a second self
Who listens and doesn't interrupt,
Or answer back. My only worry is
Whether or no he can keep a secret,
As there are things I wish I hadn't said:
It's true, she did smell, Katherine Mansfield,
But not "like a civet cat that had taken
To street-walking." Were my Horatio,
In some harsh otherworld, to absent
Him from felicity awhile and tell *my* story,
What a wounded name might live behind!

ON LETTERS

When the post comes early
    I feel cheated;
        not having it
            to look forward to now.

ON
SIR LESLIE STEPHEN

Here he is, look, in these fading kodaks:
An accomplished oarsman and intrepid
Mountaineer, as we know from the silver cups
On the mantelshelf and the alpenstock
Rusting in the hallway. These are facts.
They happened. They can be set down.
They are the granite in the landscape,
Whereas feelings and emotions—what he was
Thinking when told to: *Watch the birdie*—
Are as ephemeral and far off as rainbows.
When he died, the family gathered together
All the black-edged letters of condolence.

ON
THINGS WE'VE FORGOTTEN

Laying her hand on my arm as we walked
Through Kensington Gardens, "One should never,"
She said, and said with such quiet insistence,
"underestimate the importance of those things
We no longer remember: they being
As independent perhaps as the
Hessian smell of rain which lingers
After a short, sharp shower has passed.
Events so rarely live up to the thoughts
They give rise to." A notion I might have countered,
Had I not been so engrossed in the hope
That the soft touch of her fingertips,
As I felt them then, would ever be with me.

ON
CLIO

Sometimes we are liable to forget
Just how much we owe them: the gossip-mongers,
The diarists and the letter-writers,
(You only have to think of Walpole)
Yes, Lytton had it so right: it is they who catch up
The flashy robes of our Muse of History
And show the world her dirty underwear.

ON
REPUTATIONS

Not that I would ever dream of asking,
But you, I suppose, will know whose reputation
Has, as the saying goes, *stood the test of time*,
Or whether we've all been filtered out.
Not that it matters: the little piece of quartz
You saw me toss just now into that rock pool, will,
As we are well aware, outlast the name of Aeschylus.

ON
RAILWAY JOURNEYS

I used to think everybody did it,
For if one neglects to take a book
How else is one supposed to pass the time
On a train journey? I'll call her Elsie,
Partly because I know of no one
Of that name, and partly because there's something
In the severity of her mouth and a certain
Sallowness about her cheeks suggests it.
She lives, I would hazard, in a terraced
House in one of the outer suburbs.
I can see her now walking home one damp
November evening. She turns her key
In the lock. She lives with her mother,
An irascible—"You've left that gate
Open again"—old lady who is going bald.
She closes the door behind her, takes off
Her coat, and hurries upstairs to the toilet.
She doesn't like to use the toilets on trains.
And then—and you would not believe just how
Exasperating this is—she only goes
Two stops and gets off at Ladywell!
And then as she steps down onto the platform
I hear someone calling out, "Elaine! Elaine!"
("Elaine the fair, Elaine the loveable,
Elaine the lily maid of Astolat.")
Laughing, she runs towards him, and I feel
Her nipples stiffen when he kisses her.

ON WALKING

I know there were fewer people around
When you wrote that, "Walking alone through London
Is the greatest rest." But *rest* though? Were you
Following your father's lead when he said walking
Lets one give the mind a break and "turn it out
To play for a season"? But faced with a problem,
I am sure he would, like everyone else, have "taken steps"
To resolve it. *Solvitur ambulando*,
As someone—I forget who—once put it.
Many of our tribe, I would guess, think
And write on the hoof. I did when I hoofed it
Across Spain. And in your diary it says you wrote
"Jacob's Room" *incessantly* on your walks.
No, Sir Leslie was on far firmer ground
Celebrating, "the intellectual harmony
Which is the natural accompaniment
To the monotonous tramp of one's feet."

ON
EVENTS VERSUS IDEAS

Oh, cups and saucers are all very well;
That is, if you happen to be pouring tea,
Plates too, if you want somewhere to put your cake,
But do we really need them in our novels?
That's my point. If things are the sons of the earth
And words the daughters of heaven, what then of
Thoughts and feelings? Take that trim young woman
Sitting by herself over there now,
Wouldn't you rather learn what's going on
Inside her head than know what she's got in her
Handbag? I would; of that you may be quite sure.

ON EXPECTATION

But the great
    revelation
never did come;
    instead,
those little daily miracles:
    matches
struck unexpectedly
    in the dark.

ON
MORNINGS

Many's the morning I wake up, look around me
And announce, *"Dear God, here I am again,"*
To the still, soft-focused world.
No need for me to stir as yet though.
Floorboards creak; then footsteps,
And downstairs I hear a door slam,
The whistle of the kettle and a clattering
Of coals in the scuttle. Bright bursts
Of birdsong, and should the curtain move
A low sun comes sidling in, mimicking itself
On the brass nobs of the dresser. But listen now,
All of you, the day must come when you
Will have to undertake these little rituals without me,
But then, ah, I dare say you'll cope.

ON
PARTICULARITIES

"Observe particularities," was the advice Mr James
  Once gave me, "the actions of ordinary
  Minds on an ordinary day."
                              Did he mean
  Those shop-girls, all of a giggle on the omnibus.
  "Oh no, he didn't dare, did he?"
  The rituals of romance.
                              Or again:
  When Leonard and I took some plums
  Round to Mrs Grey this evening and found her
  Sitting on a hard chair in the corner
  Of her kitchen, with that wild expressionless
  Stare of the very old. "Every night," she said,
  I prays to God to take me."

ON
SERVANTS

A Room of One's Own. Now your cook, Nelly Boxall,
(She herself spelled it *Nellie*, by the way)
Did have one at Rodmell, but sat in it
All by herself, while through its thin walls
She could hear you and Leonard
Chatting, or listening to the wireless.
The very idea of inviting her in to sit
With you was of course quite unthinkable.
And while £500 a year you thought the least
An independent woman needed, you paid her fifty,
And wondered why she kept on giving notice.
All right, all right, I realise this isn't
Something a feminist would wish to talk about,
Save for your: "Servants, why do we bother with them?"

ON
DAYS

Henry James, so I'm told, once said
Summer afternoons were among his favourite words,
Whereas, for me, a red-admiral-
feasting-on-fallen-apples kind of day
Is my idea of perfection.

ON
THE ASSOCIATION OF IDEAS

I know what you mean:
Pausing by the mantelpiece one evening
Your eye was caught by the blue and white
China bowl you'd bought in Mantua
And how it all came back to you:
It had been a windy day; the sinister
Old woman who sold it you; and how that night
The innkeeper and his wife had quarrelled
So furiously you couldn't sleep, so got up
And leaning out of the window looked
At the stars and how bright they'd been.
You see, there's this little metal drinking cup,
Tarnished and a bit misshapen that I bought
Somewhere in Turkey—Fethiye it might have been—
What I remember is the sound of the man's footsteps
Running after me and him calling out,
"All right then, ten lira," the absurd amount
I'd offered him because I didn't really want it.
That was—what—some twenty years ago at least
And I've not been parted from it since.

ON
LYTTON STRACHEY

I do love that portrait Carrington did
Of Strachey slummocked in his deckchair
In the garden at Tidmarsh. So at ease,
Or so it would seem. It was all a pose of course.
That surprises you? Oh come, he was ever
The quintessential poseur, our Lytton.
With that floppy hat of his, the long red beard
And copious cape, he was everything the plebs
Despised, which is maybe why I loved him.
He proposed to me once, and I accepted,
But we slept on it, (no, no, not together)
Thought better of it; stayed good friends instead.

ON
COPING WITH LOSS

That something is inconceivable
Does not, I need to remind myself,
Mean that it might not be impossible.
Things happen. This thing has happened.
The loss though is by no means mine alone.
No. Together, we could (so why don't we?)
Found a movement, a silent, tender
Yet defiant protest at one more
Unique embodiment of experience having come,
And come so irrevocably, to an end.

ON
THAT VERY MOMENT

There is really no point in asking me again,
As I have not the faintest idea what
Could have brought me to say such a thing.
How she was holding her hands at that moment,
I do recall: the tips of her fingers ever so slightly apart,
As though cradling a spray of apple blossom
And fearful of crushing it—not that she was
Of course, it being late November, as I told you,
And the little daylight still left to us,
Though it caught and lit up the yellow tassels
Of the bell-pull, as it seeped through the narrow
Windows, was not enough to lift the veil
Of shadows from her face, and so,
Whether she was listening to the sonata
Sydney was practising (oh, those arpeggios)
In the drawing room, or to the starlings
Settling themselves down for the night,
Or indeed to me, there was no way of telling.
Nevertheless, it is a scene I now re-enact
To myself, as you well know, over and
Over again—yes, and word-perfectly.

ON
NOTHING IN PARTICULAR

I'd never have managed
        to get anything done,
If I hadn't been capable
        of doing nothing.

ON
LISTENING

Can't you, please, leave me alone, just for one
Moment? I'm not important. Play some Mozart;
Read some Hopkins, Eliot; me, if you must,
But do it properly and you'll find that
You are the music; you are the words.
Only think, and you are the thing itself.

ON
PEACE

Mrs Woolf, may I introduce to you
Flight Lieutenant Edmund Jeffreys, DFC,
He tells me he recently bought a copy
Of your book *The Death of the Moth*.
(I actually have it now on my own
Bookshelf, signed by him at RAF Catfoss.)
It's the collection which ends with your essay
"Thoughts on Peace in an Air Raid",
And I wondered if you might be interested
In how he reacted to the notion
That young airmen needed to root out
Their love of medals and decorations.
You'll need to hurry though, before he
Takes off again. He's due to die soon, you see:
Caught in the cross-sights of a Messerschmitt
And brought down somewhere off the coast of France.
Yes, he was twenty-three, poor man. Poor young man.

ON
AIR RAIDS

Our paths did cross once then, it would seem,
If, as you say, you remember everything going
Quiet; your mother holding you close
In her arms and looking up at a pulsating orange sky
Below which Liverpool was burning.
The same bombers might have flown over us
In Sussex, and I can well remember how silent
We all went, hearing that droning, muffled roar. No one
Spoke. All feeling, all thinking stopped; just dread.
We cowered down inside ourselves until they'd gone,
Appalled, terrified, yet curiously detached;
Then carried on with our conversations
As though nothing whatsoever had happened.

ON
WOMEN AND TWO WORLD WARS

There were just too many buggers. The word
 Shocks you, does it? I'm sorry, but there were,
With some of my closest friends among them,
And holding positions of such power
That any scheme we might have hatched to resuscitate
The Lysistrata ploy would have been a
Total waste of time. You ask Leonard;
 Not that he would have noticed, mind you.
 By the bye, I was reading *Antigone*
 Last night—no, I'm not changing the subject—
And there was Il Duce, Creon, pontificating:
"We must in no wise suffer a woman
 To worst us," so he led her to where the ways
Were loneliest and had her entombed, alive.
 Emmeline, I thought. Holloway. The hunger-strikers.
 Creon, so we read, brought ruin on his house
And scattered the land with the bodies of the dead.

ON
ENDINGS

Rooks have begun clattering about again
Up in the bare branches of the elm tree,
And from my lodge window I can see
Mr George's stately Suffolk Punch,
Slowly and steadily pulling the plough,
Each damp turve gleaming as it's turned.
A chaffinch flies down onto the hawthorn hedge.
It is spring. Some early primroses are out
And an over-wintering tortoiseshell
Comes crawling from behind my curtain.
Every little flutter though is followed by a fall.
Look. Flutter and fall. Flutter and fall. Do you see?
It's going to die. Yes, but look how it struggles.

ON
SELF-DOUBT

What if I were to walk down to the lake
One evening, and chanced upon my parents
Standing there, and bearing my entire
Life in my arms I were to say to them,
"This, this is what I made of it."? What then,
I wonder, as I unwrapped the bundle,
Would I have to show them? Words, yes words,
Far too many for them to bother with,
The friendship of some people of distinction,
A husband I had been such a trial to
And... and... but what if Father were to turn
To me, raise the severeness of his eyebrows,
And ask, "Is this it, Virginia? Is this it?"

ON
LEONARD WOOLF

I wish you could have known Leonard. Indeed,
There are times when I wish I knew him,
But sitting quietly beside him here
In our own book-lined cell in Monk's House
I thought of Julian of Norwich, alone
In hers, and wished (prayed almost) I could bring
Myself to believe, like her, that *All manner
Of thing shall be well*. For Leonard at least.
But there's a cold wind getting up outside
And the fire looks to be about to die.
One of us will have to move soon.

ON
GARDENING

While I did what I could
            while I had the time,
The rhododendrons
           I left for Leonard.

ON
WALKING BY THE RIVER

It was not, and of this she was quite sure,
A river-walk she had ever taken before,
Hence this altogether-unlooked-for familiarity,
This attunement, one might call it, was something
Of a puzzle. Her senses were not only
Reaching out, she felt, but were in turn,
Or so it seemed, being reached for, sought.
"The sacrament of the present moment."
Now where was it she'd come across those words?
It was only later, when sitting quietly
Down by the weir that she saw the kingfisher.

*I like to go out of the room talking,
with an unfinished casual sentence on my lips.*